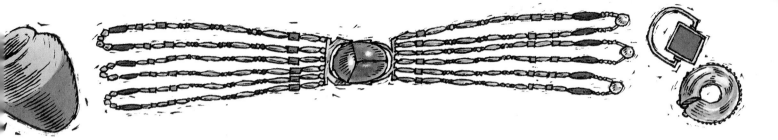

THE FACTS ABOUT

THE
EGYPTIANS

Jen Green

HODDER
Wayland

an imprint of Hodder Children's Books

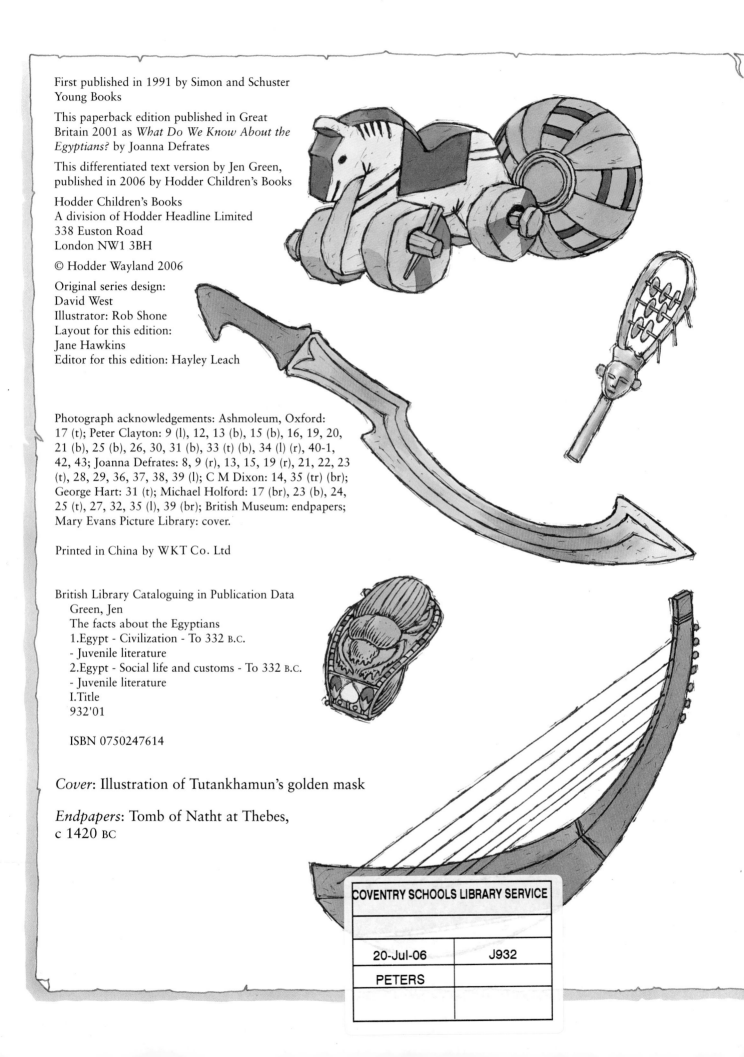

First published in 1991 by Simon and Schuster
Young Books

This paperback edition published in Great
Britain 2001 as *What Do We Know About the
Egyptians?* by Joanna Defrates

This differentiated text version by Jen Green,
published in 2006 by Hodder Children's Books

Hodder Children's Books
A division of Hodder Headline Limited
338 Euston Road
London NW1 3BH

© Hodder Wayland 2006

Original series design:
David West
Illustrator: Rob Shone
Layout for this edition:
Jane Hawkins
Editor for this edition: Hayley Leach

Photograph acknowledgements: Ashmoleum, Oxford:
17 (t); Peter Clayton: 9 (l), 12, 13 (b), 15 (b), 16, 19, 20,
21 (b), 25 (b), 26, 30, 31 (b), 33 (t) (b), 34 (l) (r), 40-1,
42, 43; Joanna Defrates: 8, 9 (r), 13, 15, 19 (r), 21, 22, 23
(t), 28, 29, 36, 37, 38, 39 (l); C M Dixon: 14, 35 (tr) (br);
George Hart: 31 (t); Michael Holford: 17 (br), 23 (b), 24,
25 (t), 27, 32, 35 (l), 39 (br); British Museum: endpapers;
Mary Evans Picture Library: cover.

Printed in China by WKT Co. Ltd

British Library Cataloguing in Publication Data
    Green, Jen
    The facts about the Egyptians
    1.Egypt - Civilization - To 332 B.C.
    - Juvenile literature
    2.Egypt - Social life and customs - To 332 B.C.
    - Juvenile literature
    I.Title
    932'01

    ISBN 0750247614

Cover: Illustration of Tutankhamun's golden mask

Endpapers: Tomb of Natht at Thebes,
c 1420 BC

CONTENTS

Words that appear in **bold** can be found in the glossary on page 44.

WHO WERE THE EGYPTIANS?

About 7,000 years ago, one of the world's greatest civilisations grew up along the River Nile in Egypt. Every year, the Nile flooded, covering the land with rich, black mud. Crops grew well in the fertile soil.

▼ PLANTS OF EGYPT

The **papyrus** and lotus (pictured on the temples below) are symbols of Egypt. Lotus grew in the river valley, papyrus near the sea.

▼ TWO LANDS

Egypt was originally two separate kingdoms. The land along the river valley in the south was Upper Egypt. Lower Egypt lay on the marshy **delta** in the north. In about 3100 BC, a ruler named King Menes united the two kingdoms. Later Egyptian rulers were called 'Lord of the Two Lands'.

ALONG THE RIVER ▶

Empty desert stretched out on either side of the River Nile, but the narrow strip of land along the river was suitable for farming. Food was plentiful, so there was spare time to develop arts and crafts, writing, music and wonderful buildings.

▼ EGYPTIAN PEOPLE

In Egyptian art, women are shown with fairer skin than men. They probably spent more time indoors. Egyptians were fairly short with straight black hair. This woman is wearing a wig.

HOW DO WE KNOW? ▶

The Egyptians wrote in picture symbols called **hieroglyphs**. For a long time, no one could read Egyptian writing. Then in 1822, a clever French scholar cracked the code.

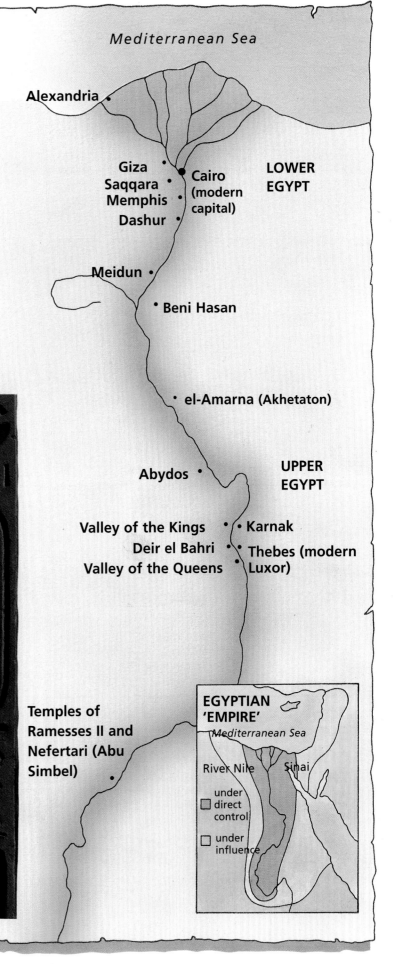

Mediterranean Sea

Alexandria

Giza
Saqqara   Cairo
Memphis   (modern
Dashur   capital)

LOWER
EGYPT

Meidun

Beni Hasan

el-Amarna (Akhetaton)

Abydos

UPPER
EGYPT

Valley of the Kings   Karnak
Deir el Bahri   Thebes (modern
Valley of the Queens   Luxor)

Temples of
Ramesses II and
Nefertari (Abu
Simbel)

EGYPTIAN
'EMPIRE'
Mediterranean Sea

River Nile   Sinai

☐ under
direct
control

☐ under
influence

TIMELINE

BC	3000	2700	2400	2100	1800	1500
EVENTS IN EGYPT	Egypt is unified. Art and writing develop. **Double crown**	Imhotep is Chancellor. The pyramids and sphinx are built.	First *obelisks* are built.	The Old Kingdom ends. Queen Kawit rules c. 2030 BC. Middle Kingdom begins c. 2000 BC	Smaller brick pyramids are built, with planned towns around them. Middle Kingdom ends in c. 1650 BC.	New Kingdom begins. Huge temples are built at Karnak and Luxor (Thebes). The capital moves to Amarna, but Tutankhamun returns it to Thebes.
PHARAOHS AND RULERS	Menes or Narmer unites Egypt. **King Narmur**	Time of the great pyramid builders: Djoser, Sneferu, Khufu, Khafre and Menkaure.	Unas is the first **pharaoh** to have writing inside his pyramid. Pepi rules for over 90 years. The first queen rules.	A time of unrest ends when Mentuhotep, prince of Thebes, reunites Egypt.	Senwosret and Amenemhat are great pharaohs. The Hyksos people from Asia invade Egypt.	A prince of Thebes reunites Egypt. New Kingdom rulers include Tuthmosis III, Queen Hatshepsut, Tutankhamun and Queen Nefertiti.
CONTACT WITH OTHER LANDS	Possible contacts with the eastern Mediterranean and Red Sea.	Trade with the Middle East and African nations south of Egypt.	Expeditions to Nubia and the Sudan.	After the Old Kingdom ends, Egypt is divided into smaller states ruled by petty kings.	Nubia is conquered, and forts are built along the Upper Nile. **scimitar**	The Hyksos from Asia invade, but are driven out. Later Nubia is reconquered, as are Syria and Palestine. Great expansion of Egypt.
EVENTS AROUND THE WORLD	The first towns grow up in Mesopotamia in Asia. Writing is invented. **Stonehenge**	Civilisation develops at Ur in Asia. Building of Stonehenge begins in Britain.	The Indus civilisation develops in Pakistan.	Stonehenge is finished. Babylonian civilisation develops in Asia.	The Hittite empire grows in Asia. Minoan civilisation develops on Crete.	Minoan civilisation fails after a tidal wave caused by an eruption hits Crete.

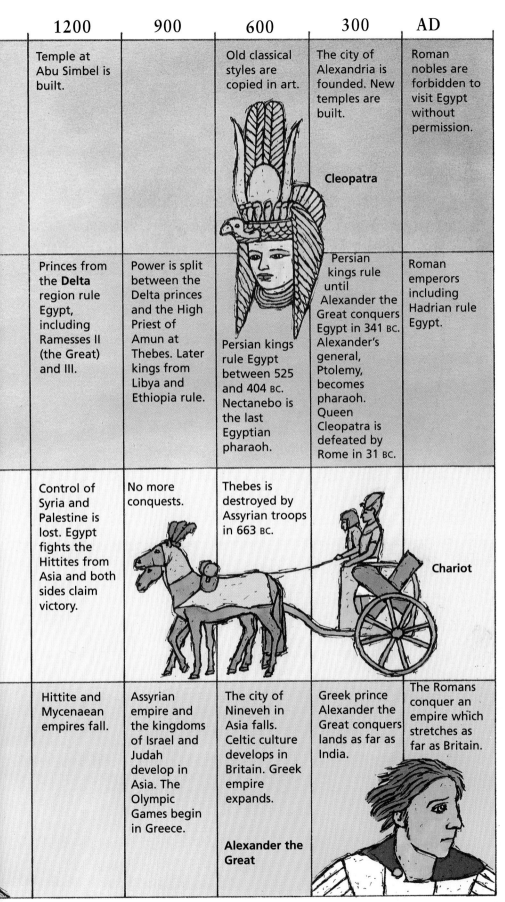

1200	900	600	300	AD
Temple at Abu Simbel is built.		Old classical styles are copied in art.	The city of Alexandria is founded. New temples are built.	Roman nobles are forbidden to visit Egypt without permission.
Princes from the **Delta** region rule Egypt, including Ramesses II (the Great) and III.	Power is split between the Delta princes and the High Priest of Amun at Thebes. Later kings from Libya and Ethiopia rule.	Persian kings rule Egypt between 525 and 404 BC. Nectanebo is the last Egyptian pharaoh.	Persian kings rule until Alexander the Great conquers Egypt in 341 BC. Alexander's general, Ptolemy, becomes pharaoh. Queen Cleopatra is defeated by Rome in 31 BC.	Roman emperors including Hadrian rule Egypt.
Control of Syria and Palestine is lost. Egypt fights the Hittites from Asia and both sides claim victory.	No more conquests.	Thebes is destroyed by Assyrian troops in 663 BC.		
Hittite and Mycenaean empires fall.	Assyrian empire and the kingdoms of Israel and Judah develop in Asia. The Olympic Games begin in Greece.	The city of Nineveh in Asia falls. Celtic culture develops in Britain. Greek empire expands.	Greek prince Alexander the Great conquers lands as far as India.	The Romans conquer an empire which stretches as far as Britain.

Cleopatra

Chariot

Alexander the Great

EGYPT'S HISTORY

Egypt's long history is divided into three main periods called kingdoms. Weak kings ruled in times of unrest between the Old, Middle and New Kingdoms. A line of pharaohs is called a **dynasty**. The title of pharaoh passed from a king to his son or heir.

Predynastic Egypt
5000–3100 BC
Old Kingdom
c. 2500–2100 BC
First Intermediate Period
Middle Kingdom
c. 2000–1650 BC
Second Intermediate Period
New Kingdom
c. 1550–1100 BC
Third Intermediate Period
Late period c. 700–332 BC
Greek and Roman period
332 BC–395 AD

BC OR AD?

We count dates from the year Jesus Christ was born. AD or *Anno Domini* means 'in the year of our Lord'. Years before Christ (BC) are counted backwards.

HOW DID THE EGYPTIANS FARM?

Farming provided much of Egypt's wealth. The yearly flood made the soil fertile. Each summer, river water spilled over the fields, leaving

rich, black soil. Farmers planted their crops in autumn, ready for harvest the following spring. Everyone helped at harvest time. Wheat and barley were grown to make bread and beer. Flax fibres were woven to make linen cloth.

▼ HARVEST TIME

This painting from a tomb shows farming methods. The farmer cuts the corn with a wooden sickle with sharp stone teeth. His wife follows, gathering the crop in a basket. However, the painting is not very realistic. The couple are shown wearing their best clothes and wigs, which would not happen at harvest time!

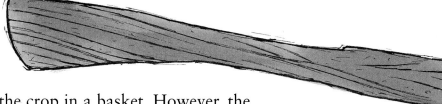

▼ PLOUGH

Wooden ploughs turned the soil. They were pulled by cattle or people.

Plough

▲ FERTILE FIELDS

When the flood waters went down, people channelled river water to wet their fields. This process is called irrigation. Three thousand years ago an Egyptian wrote of his home: 'Its fields are full of good things… Its ponds are full of fish and its lakes full of birds. He who lives there is happy…'

Shadduf

▼ ANIMALS

As well as cattle to pull ploughs, farmers also kept sheep, goats, pigs, horses, geese and ducks. Horses were not used on the land – they were too valuable.

▲ LIFTING WATER

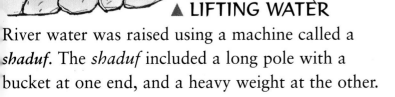

River water was raised using a machine called a *shaduf*. The *shaduf* included a long pole with a bucket at one end, and a heavy weight at the other.

DAMMING THE NILE

A huge dam called the Aswan Dam was built on the Nile in modern times. The river no longer floods to leave rich mud, so farmers now have to add fertiliser to the soil instead.

13

DID THE EGYPTIANS EAT WELL?

The Egyptians loved good food and drink. Even poor people ate a healthy diet of fish, bread, fruit and vegetables. Wealthy people gave huge banquets. Guests sometimes ate and drank so much roast meat, cakes, fruit and wine they made themselves sick! Food was eaten with the fingers.

BREAD AND SWEETS ▶

Bread was the basic food of ordinary people. It was made from grain, which was stored in barns called granaries to keep it fresh. When it was ground to make flour, a little sand may have been added to help the grinding. The gritty mixture was very bad for teeth. The Egyptians also loved sweet foods. Bakers made many kinds of bread and rolls sweetened with nuts and honey. Balls of chopped dates and walnuts, coated with honey and almonds, were popular. No wonder people got toothache!

◀ COUNTING GEESE

The official on the left is counting geese and eggs so he knows how much tax is owed.

14

In the hot climate of Egypt, it was important to preserve meat so it did not turn bad. Duck and fish were dried in the sun. Salt was added to fish to preserve it. This wall carving shows servants salting fish.

FOOD AND DRINK

As well as wheat and barley, farmers grew lentils, beans, onions, garlic, leeks, cucumber and lettuce. Dates, figs and pomegranates were grown in orchards. Both dates and grapes were used to make wine. Farmers also kept bees for honey, which was used to sweeten food.

WHAT WERE EGYPTIAN FAMILIES LIKE?

Egyptian families were a lot like ours, but bigger. Most people had many children. That way, at least some children would survive to carry on the family business and look after parents when they were old. Egyptians married young: girls at about 12, boys at 14. Parents decided who their children married. Girls stayed at home until they were married.

WHO GOT MARRIED?

Egyptians often married members of their own family. Uncles married nieces, or two cousins would marry. You could get a divorce, but it was expensive.

▼ FAMILY LIFE

This tomb painting shows Inhirkha, a foreman who worked on royal tombs, with his wife, son and grandchildren. The children are playing with their pet birds. Inhirkha must be quite old, but he is shown here in the prime of life.

▼ YOUNG PRINCESSES

This painting shows two of the six daughters of Queen Nefertiti. The girls are shown sitting on an embroidered cushion, and are drawn in the style of the time.

Wooden horse

Ball

Knucklebone

Wooden lion

 LONG LIVES?

Egyptians lived to about 40 years on average. However, records claim one king ruled for 67 years, and another ruled for an amazing 96 years!

TOYS AND GAMES

Egyptian boys and girls played with balls, dolls, spinning tops and wooden animals. They also played a game with knucklebones: throwing them in the air and trying to catch them on the back of one hand.

PETS ▼

Cats and dogs were the most common pets, but some families had a pet monkey or even a tame deer. Dogs were used for hunting, and also by the army and police.

WHAT WERE EGYPTIAN HOUSES LIKE?

Most buildings in Egypt were made of mud bricks, dried and hardened in the sun. Few ordinary houses have survived into modern times, though stone temples have lasted well. Poor people lived in homes with just one room for living, eating and sleeping. Rich people lived in bigger houses with two or three storeys. Town houses were built close together. Many wealthy people preferred to live in the country, in villas surrounded by gardens and shady pools.

Folding stool

▲ A TOWN HOUSE

This drawing shows the town house of a rich official. Servants carry water up an outside staircase to a kitchen on the roof. Other servants weave cloth in the basement. On the first floor, the official's wife offers him a drink.

FURNITURE ▼

Egyptian homes contained less furniture than modern homes. Wealthy people had low tables, carved chairs and folding stools. Servants and poorer people sat on mats or cushions on the floor.

Oil lamp on stand

Three-legged table

Chair

Headrest

FINDING OUT ABOUT HOUSES ▼

What we know about Egyptian houses mostly comes from paintings and models found in tombs. Villages are difficult to **excavate** because new houses were often built on top of old ones. Workers who built royal tombs lived in villages like this one. Each house had a flat roof and a small yard.

◄A COUNTRY HOUSE

Vents on the roof of this villa catch cool breezes. The bricks are covered with plaster and a coat of whitewash.

 POPULATION

The city of Memphis, Egypt's capital, contained about 500,000 people. Up to four million people lived in the whole country.

DID CHILDREN GO TO SCHOOL?

We don't know much about Egyptian schools as there are no pictures of them. Boys were taught at boarding schools linked to temples or they learned from wise men. In poorer families, fathers taught sons to do their work. Girls did not go to school, but learned cooking, spinning and weaving at home. However, some girls could read and write.

▼ SCRIBES

Egypt was run using detailed records written by scribes. Some **scribes** went on to become priests, doctors or officials.

▼ LETTERS AND NUMBERS

Children learned to read by chanting words and phrases aloud. They copied letters onto flakes of stone – **papyrus** was too costly. Egyptian numbering was based on tens, but there were no numbers for 2 to 9. So 35 was written:

10+10+10+1+1+1+1+1.

10 = ∩

1 = |

100 = ℰ

1000 = ₰

So 42 = ∩ ∩ |
∩ ∩ |

Scribe writing

Papyrus rolls

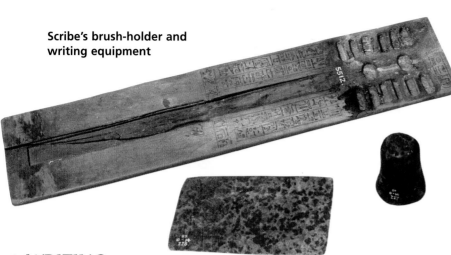

Scribe's brush-holder and writing equipment

WHICH WAY?

Writing could be read from left to right or right to left. You read from the direction the figures faced.

Papyrus plant

▲ WRITING

Egyptians developed their writing system around 3,000 BC. The script is made up of small pictures called **hieroglyphs**. Each picture stands for an object and a sound, or one or more letters. Only consonants are shown, not vowels. For everyday business, people used a simpler script. This was more like modern handwriting, with letters joined together.

TOMB WRITING ▼

Writing could also run vertically or horizontally. Straight lines show these columns run downwards.

MAKING PAPER ▼

Paper was made from the stem of the papyrus reed that grew by the Nile. The inner stem or **pith** was sliced, and the strips laid lengthways and crossways. This was then squashed flat to make a sheet of paper. Sheets were fixed together to make rolls.

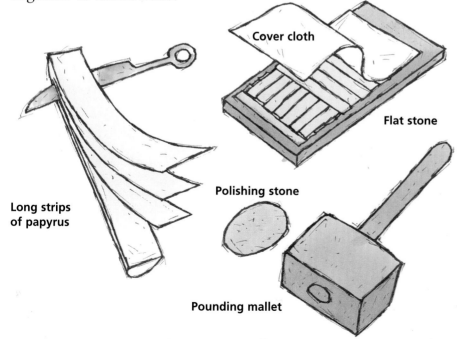

Cover cloth

Flat stone

Polishing stone

Long strips of papyrus

Pounding mallet

21

WHAT WORK DID PEOPLE DO?

In theory, everyone in Egypt worked for the pharaoh. In practice, farmers worked the land and paid tax to the king. Builders and craftsmen worked for the government or temples. Big projects like the pyramids needed architects, craftsmen and thousands of labourers.

Bow drill

Chisel

Awl

Adze

Winnowing fan

Wooden sickle

▲ QUEEN'S TEMPLE

Queen Hatshepsut ruled Egypt from about 1473 to 1453 BC. Her temple (shown above) was one of the most spectacular buildings in Egypt. Priests performed rituals here when she died. Built into a mountain, the temple was once brightly painted, with gardens in front. Statues of the queen stood on the terrace.

▲ TOOLS

Tools used by Egyptian carpenters were similar to modern tools. Axes, **adzes**, chisels, drills, **awls** and hammers were made of bronze, but other metals are used today.

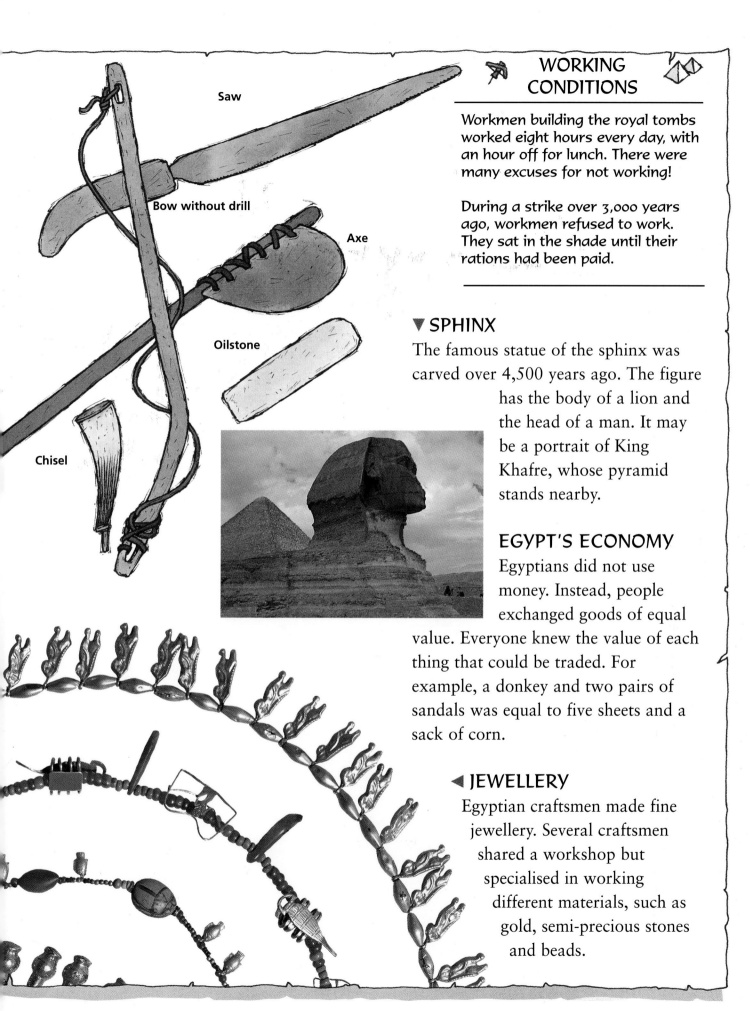

Saw

Bow without drill

Axe

Oilstone

Chisel

Workmen building the royal tombs worked eight hours every day, with an hour off for lunch. There were many excuses for not working!

During a strike over 3,000 years ago, workmen refused to work. They sat in the shade until their rations had been paid.

▼ SPHINX

The famous statue of the sphinx was carved over 4,500 years ago. The figure has the body of a lion and the head of a man. It may be a portrait of King Khafre, whose pyramid stands nearby.

EGYPT'S ECONOMY

Egyptians did not use money. Instead, people exchanged goods of equal value. Everyone knew the value of each thing that could be traded. For example, a donkey and two pairs of sandals was equal to five sheets and a sack of corn.

◀ JEWELLERY

Egyptian craftsmen made fine jewellery. Several craftsmen shared a workshop but specialised in working different materials, such as gold, semi-precious stones and beads.

WHAT DID PEOPLE DO IN THEIR FREE TIME?

The Egyptians did not have yearly holidays like us, but no work was done during religious festivals. Eventually festivals took up about a third of the year, so people had plenty of time off! Hunting was a popular pastime for well-off people. After chariots pulled by horses were invented, kings and noblemen hunted lions. They even hunted hippos using lassoes and harpoons.

HUNTING ▶

Fishing and hunting birds were popular pastimes. Regular fishermen used traps and nets, but noblemen killed birds with throwing sticks. This painting shows a nobleman called Nebamun hunting birds with his family. A cat is shown fetching a wounded bird. The painting is not very realistic, as all three people are wearing their best clothes!

FESTIVALS ▼

Religious festivals were a time of celebration. Statues of the gods were paraded through the streets. There was music, dancing, acrobats, jugglers and feasts, and people drank a lot of wine. Noblemen gave private banquets for their friends. This painting shows a feast given by Nebamun. Male and female guests usually sat separately.

ENTERTAINMENT

Wrestling, athletics and gymnastic contests provided entertainment. Boys showed off their skill and strength at such contests. Girls sang and did acrobatic dances.

Story-telling was popular in cold weather. There were exciting tales of magic, ghosts and adventure. Cinderella is an Egyptian story. Another tale concerned a shipwrecked sailor, like Sinbad the Sailor.

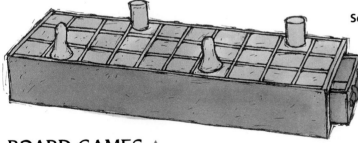

Senet board and pieces

BOARD GAMES ▲

Egyptians loved a board game called **senet**. It was played with counters and was similar to backgammon. The aim was to get all your pieces off the board before the other player. Egyptians did not have dice. Instead, people threw special sticks, that were round on one side and flat on the other. Tomb paintings, like this one, often show people playing senet.

WHAT DID THE EGYPTIANS WEAR?

Light, cool clothing was vital in a hot country like Egypt. Flax plants produced fibres which were woven to make linen. Men wore short kilts, women simple shift dresses. Later, pleated dresses and tunics became fashionable. Both men and women wore jewellery. Egyptians wore sandals made of reeds or leather on their feet.

PLAITING HAIR ▼

A carving on the tomb of Queen Kawit shows a maid plaiting the queen's hair. Both women are wearing simple, elegant dresses. The queen has beautiful jewellery. Her mirror is made of polished bronze.

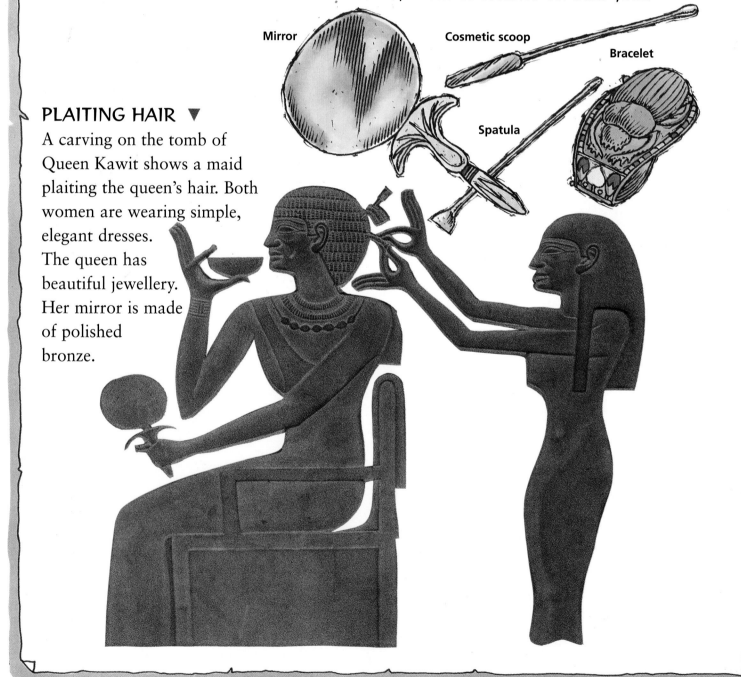

Mirror

Cosmetic scoop

Bracelet

Spatula

WIGS AND PERFUME ▲

Ladies wore cones of perfumed fat on their wigs at banquets. As the fat melted in the heat, the perfumed oil would run down the wig.

Comb

Kohl pot

Pot for cosmetics

Shawl

Curly-toed sandal

HAIRSTYLES ▲

Egyptian men and women often shaved their heads as well as their bodies. Children had shaved heads apart from a long lock of hair. Men and women wore wigs in public. Long, heavy wigs were worn on special occasions, but even these were made to be cool and comfortable.

Bronze razor

Amulet

 MAKEUP

Both women and men wore makeup including eyeliner, called kohl, made from finely ground minerals. Women painted their lips and cheeks with red clay.

Oil was used to soften the skin before shaving. There was no soap. Women used cleansing creams and body scrubs.

PLEATED CLOTHES

No one knows how Egyptians managed to pleat their clothes so beautifully. Servants may have pressed the damp cloth into a grooved board to get the pleats.

WHO DID THE EGYPTIANS WORSHIP?

Religion was very important in ancient Egypt. It helped people understand the world around them and cope with problems and difficulties. People believed in many different gods and goddesses who each controlled one part of daily life. Every town or village had a god that protected it. Most people had an altar at home, or a chapel in the garden, where they prayed. On religious festivals everyone went to the temple.

OFFERINGS ▼

This painting shows the **pharaoh** making an offering to the god Horus, who protected kings. Every god or goddess was associated with a particular animal.

In paintings and carvings they are often shown with that animal's head. The sky god Horus is shown with a falcon's head.

1 Montu – god of war
2 Amun – creator god
3 Thoth – god of writing
4 Khons – god of the moon
5 Horus – royal protector
6 Sekhmet – goddess of war
7 Sobek – crocodile god
8 Anubis – god of Necropolis
9 Isis – goddess of women
10 Osiris – god of death and rebirth
11 Hathor – goddess of love

1

2

3

4 **5**

CREATOR GOD ▼

This statue shows the pharaoh under the protection of Amun, the creator. This god looked after the king and all of Egypt.

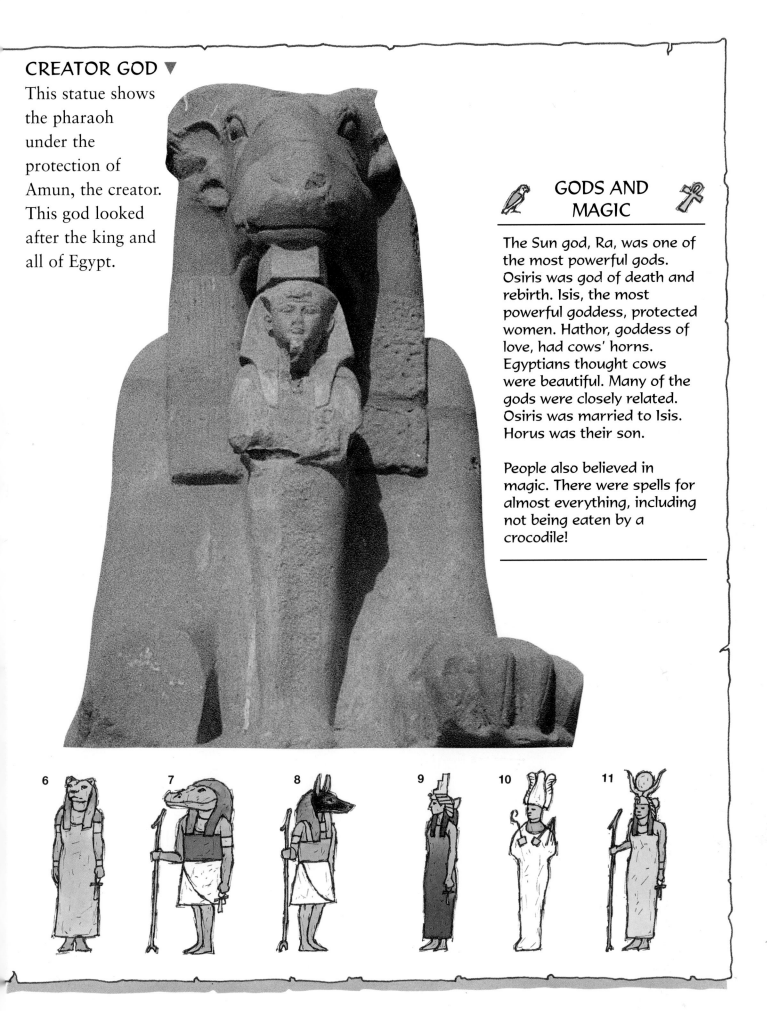

GODS AND MAGIC

The Sun god, Ra, was one of the most powerful gods. Osiris was god of death and rebirth. Isis, the most powerful goddess, protected women. Hathor, goddess of love, had cows' horns. Egyptians thought cows were beautiful. Many of the gods were closely related. Osiris was married to Isis. Horus was their son.

People also believed in magic. There were spells for almost everything, including not being eaten by a crocodile!

6 7 8 9 10 11

WHAT DID PEOPLE BELIEVE ABOUT DEATH?

Egyptians believed that when people died, a part called the soul lived on. They spent a lot of time and effort preparing carefully for death and the

life to come. It was important to preserve the physical body, so it did not decay. Without a physical body, you had no chance of life after death. So the Egyptians developed the process of embalming, or mummification.

BURIALS ▼

In the early days of Egypt, burials were simple. Bodies were laid in the sandy

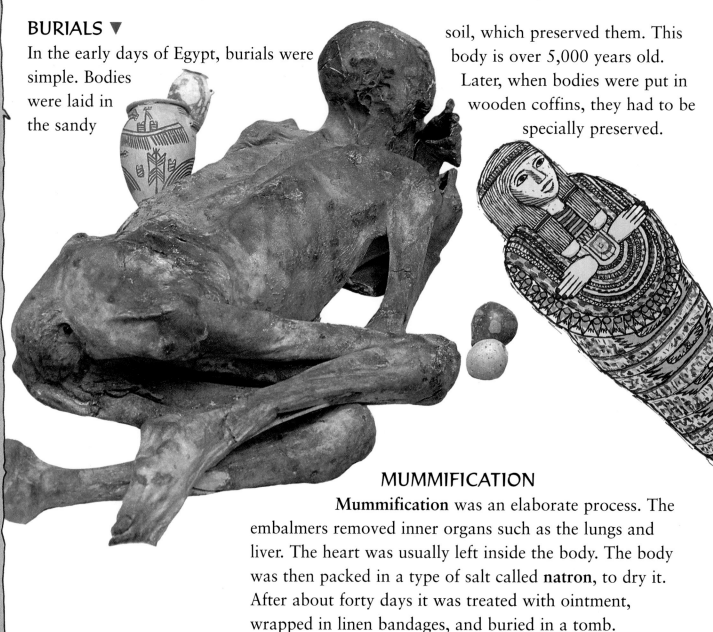

soil, which preserved them. This body is over 5,000 years old. Later, when bodies were put in wooden coffins, they had to be specially preserved.

MUMMIFICATION

Mummification was an elaborate process. The embalmers removed inner organs such as the lungs and liver. The heart was usually left inside the body. The body was then packed in a type of salt called **natron,** to dry it. After about forty days it was treated with ointment, wrapped in linen bandages, and buried in a tomb.

FUNERALS ▲

When someone died, the whole family went to the funeral. Paid mourners went too, as shown in this painting. They wailed and put dust on their heads in sorrow. Servants put furniture, clothes and even food in the tomb, as these might be needed in the afterlife.

AFTER DEATH

The Egyptians believed everyone had a spirit called a 'ba', and a 'ka' (a spirit double), as well as a physical body.

Kings were buried in secure tombs. But tomb robbers broke into the royal tombs to steal gold and jewels. All the known royal tombs had been robbed by 1,000 BC.

Gold face of King Tutankhamun

EMBALMING ▶

Anubis was the god of **embalming**. He is shown with a jackal's head.

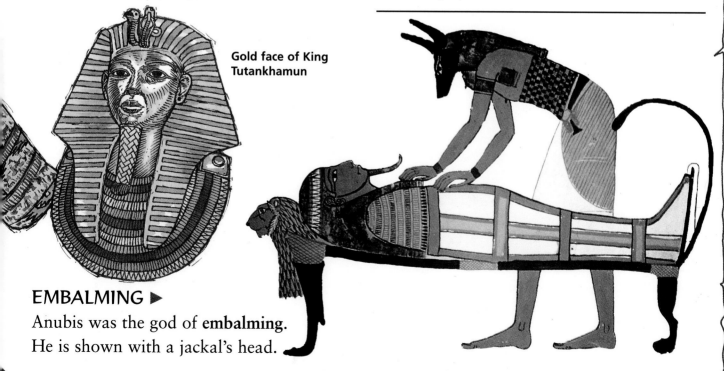

31

WHO RULED EGYPT?

The pharaoh ruled all of Egypt. In about 3100 BC, King Menes united the two kingdoms of Egypt. After this date, pharaohs wore a double crown – the white crown of Upper Egypt, and the red crown of Lower Egypt. The king appointed governors called viziers, and hundreds of other officials, to run the country in his name.

▼ MIGHTY PHARAOH

Ramesses II, pictured below, was a great **pharaoh**. He reigned for over 60 years and ordered some of Egypt's finest buildings, such as the tomb of Abu Simbel.

PRIESTS

Priests made offerings to the gods on behalf of the pharaoh. The chief priests were wealthy and powerful. Eventually they became even more powerful than the king, and ruled the whole country in his name.

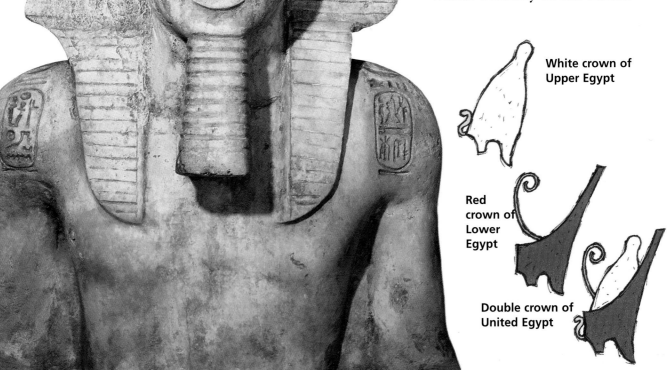

White crown of Upper Egypt

Red crown of Lower Egypt

Double crown of United Egypt

TOP JOB ▶

Amenophis, overseer of the king's works, was a top official. He is shown here as a scribe, but he was also an architect and a military commander.

GOD OR HUMAN?

At various times in history, people thought of the pharaoh as a god, the son of a god, a mighty warrior, and a good shepherd who looked after his people. We know of many instructions given about how to be a good ruler: 'Promote your officials and pay them well so they will not be tempted to take bribes... Do not prefer the well-born [man] to the commoner. Choose a man on account of his ability.'

▼ PAYING TAXES

Many officials were needed to run the country smoothly. People paid tax on their possessions. This painting shows a nobleman's cattle being counted, to work out what tax he owed.

✕ KINGS' NAMES ✋

The word pharaoh means 'great house', which is like calling the ruler 'Buckingham Palace'. Every king had a total of five names. We use the fifth name.

WERE THE EGYPTIANS ARTISTS?

The Egyptians produced wonderful paintings, sculpture, jewellery and furniture. Craftsmen didn't usually sign their work. Art was meant to last forever, so artists gave an ideal view of their subject, rather than showing faults or emotions. Most of the finest art was sealed away in tombs.

DRAWING ▼

Artists made careful drawings before beginning a painting. A grid of squares was drawn first, to make sure the proportions were right. There were also rules about drawing. People were usually shown from the side, but their eyes were shown from the front. Important people were drawn larger than less important ones.

SCULPTURE ▼

This sculpture shows the royal tutor, Seneb, and his family. The artist has made Seneb's children tiny, so they fit in the space below his legs.

◄ IN PROPORTION

This wooden drawing board, marked with a grid, shows a seated king.

The finest craftsmen worked on the royal tombs. Egyptians were skilled at using gold. This picture appears on the back of Pharaoh Tutankhamun's throne. Precious stones have been set into the gold to colour the image. Natural materials were used to colour wall paintings like the one shown below.

Egyptian colours
Black   Charcoal
White   Gypsum or calcium carbonate
Red   Ochre or iron oxide
Blue   Copper or lapis lazuli (a precious stone)
Green   Copper chloride

TOMBS AND TREASURE ▶

The Egyptians were the first people to build in stone. Their architects were very skillful. Some of the early kings were buried in huge pyramids. By the time of Tutankhamun, the pyramids were 2,000 years old. They were already tourist attractions. Tutankhamun's tomb was buried under another tomb, so it was not ransacked by robbers. Treasures such as the king's golden mask survived.

DID THE EGYPTIANS LIKE MUSIC?

Music was part of everyday life in ancient Egypt. Musicians and also dancers, acrobats, storytellers and magicians performed at religious festivals and private banquets. Some of the instruments they played are shown here.

SONG AND DANCE ▼

Professional musicians and dancing girls put on a show at banquets. Below is another scene from Nebamun's tomb. The female musicians are fashionably dressed, with perfume cones and earrings. They play the double flute and **castanets** while the dancers perform.

Bells

Lute

Oboes

Tambourine

MUSICAL INSTRUMENTS ▼

Tambourines, castanets, bells and cymbals kept time in Egyptian orchestras. Wind instruments included flutes and clarinets. Stringed instruments such as harps, lutes and lyres were also played. Tutankhamun's tomb contained ceremonial trumpets. No one is sure what Egyptian music sounded like, but it probably had a strong rhythm that made it good for dancing to.

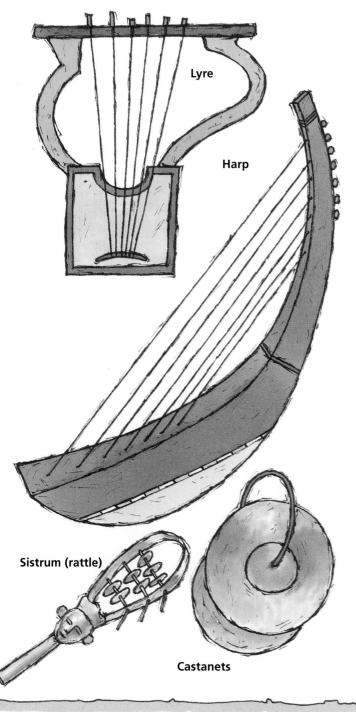

Lyre

Harp

Sistrum (rattle)

Castanets

▼ BES

Bes, the dwarf god, protected families and newborn babies. In paintings he is often shown dancing, as he was believed to be a happy god.

A BANQUET SONG

Banquet songs encouraged people to be carefree and happy:

'Follow your heart as long as you live...
Make a holiday
Don't be weary
No one can take his worldly goods with him
None who departs this life comes back again.'

 DANCING

Dancers and acrobats performed at public festivals and private parties. Dancing was more graceful at banquets. Many dancers could sing and play at the same time.

WERE THE EGYPTIANS INVENTORS?

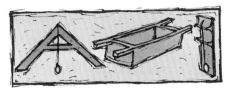

The Egyptians were skilled astronomers, doctors and dentists. They were also great architects and builders. The pyramids at Giza (seen below) rank as one of the most amazing building feats of all time. Most of the greatest building projects were completed early in Egypt's history, during the Old Kingdom. This was called 'the time of the gods'.

ARCHITECTS

The architects and engineers who built the pyramids made very accurate measurements. A tool called the plumb level made sure vertical surfaces were straight. The right angle checked if surfaces were level. If the surface was flat, the weight **bisected** the right angle.

Plumb level

Right angle

PYRAMIDS ▼

The first pyramid built at Giza had stepped sides. Later pyramids were straight-sided. The pyramids were originally covered with a layer of beautiful white limestone, but this was later stolen and used to build the city of Cairo!

▼ SHIFTING STONES

The huge blocks of stone for the pyramids were dragged on sledges pulled by oxen or teams of men. Water poured on the ground made the sledges slide more easily. The stones were hauled up temporary ramps to the upper levels. Later the ramps were removed.

Stone slab being pulled up a hill on a sledge

◄ OBELISKS

The tall column on the left is called an **obelisk**. It was cut from a single block of granite and stands 29.5 metres high. Workers took seven months to cut it from the quarry at Aswan. It was then floated down the River Nile.

FACTS AND FIGURES

• The Great Pyramid was made up of 2.3 million blocks of limestone. Each block weighed over 2.5 tonnes!

• The Great Pyramid took 20 years to build. It was finished in 2565 BC.

• Imhotep, the architect who designed the first pyramid at Giza, was later worshipped as a god.

MAKING PLANS ▼

Architects drew up detailed plans before work began on any major building project. Each measurement and angle was carefully calculated, on plans like the one shown below.

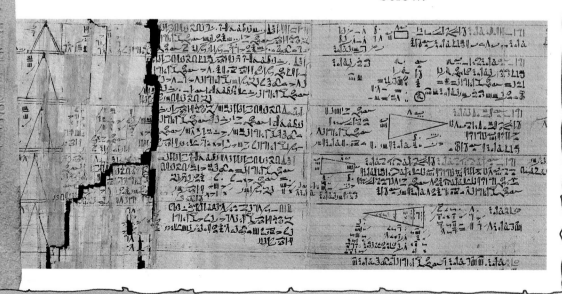

HOW DID PEOPLE TRAVEL?

The River Nile acted as Egypt's main road. Except for short journeys on foot or donkey, everything went by boat. Officials, tax collectors and traders travelled on business. Landowners visited their estates, and the whole royal court moved from Memphis to Karnak for religious occasions. However, most Egyptians didn't go abroad unless they had to. Other lands had different customs, and travel was dangerous. It was better to stay at home if you could!

BOATS ▼ ▶

Boats were used for fishing, travel, and to transport heavy cargoes such as grain and stone. The first boats were made of **papyrus** reeds and powered by oars. Later, sails were invented, and wood was used to make stronger boats.

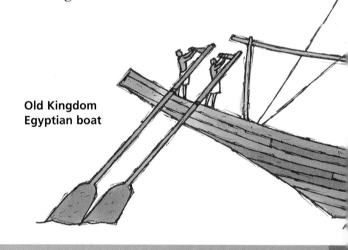

Old Kingdom Egyptian boat

TRAVEL TO NUBIA

The wealthy land of Nubia to the south attracted Egyptian explorers and traders. Traders went there to exchange luxury goods from Egypt for Nubian gold, ivory, ebony, wood, leopard skins and even live monkeys and leopards.

RIVER TRAVEL

The River Nile flows north to the sea. Egyptian boats sailed south with the wind. The current carried them north again.

The Egyptian word 'to sail' means to go south. The word for 'downstream' meant north.

When Egyptians discovered the Euphrates River in Asia, they called it the 'upside-down river' because it flowed in the opposite direction to the Nile.

TRADE WITH SYRIA ▼

Egypt also traded with eastern countries such as Syria. The painting below shows Syrians arriving to trade. With their colourful clothes, beards and leather boots, the Syrians looked very different to the Egyptians. You can see the animals, tools, weapons and furniture they have brought to trade.

DID EGYPT HAVE AN ARMY?

For most of Egypt's history, the country did not need an army. The sea and the desert protected Egypt from foreign invasion. The king had his own bodyguard, and some nobles had armies. In later times, foreign countries became jealous of Egypt's wealth, so an army was needed. Egyptian soldiers carried spears and shields, and later armour, daggers, axes and flint - or bronze-tipped arrows.

CAVALRY

By the time of Tutankhamun, around 1350 BC, the Egyptian army included mounted cavalry. Chariots were light and easy to steer. They carried two soldiers – one to shoot and one to steer.

INTO BATTLE ▼

This painting shows Tutankhamun riding into battle. The enemy, an Asian army, has been **routed**, while the Egyptians are still in neat lines. The **pharaoh** wears a blue war crown. The artist has left out his **charioteer**.

Scimitar

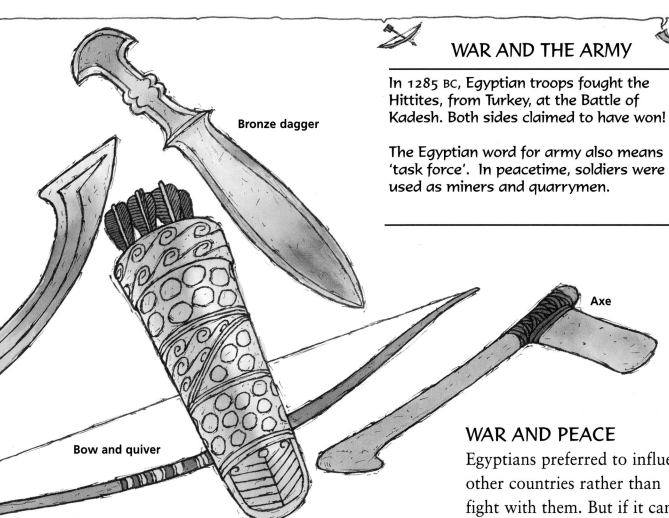

Bronze dagger

Bow and quiver

Axe

WAR AND THE ARMY

In 1285 BC, Egyptian troops fought the Hittites, from Turkey, at the Battle of Kadesh. Both sides claimed to have won!

The Egyptian word for army also means 'task force'. In peacetime, soldiers were used as miners and quarrymen.

MODEL ARMY ▼

Some top officials and noblemen had private armies. Model soldiers like these were sometimes put in tombs, in case they were needed in the afterlife.

WAR AND PEACE

Egyptians preferred to influence other countries rather than fight with them. But if it came to war, they could be ruthless. Prisoners often had one hand cut off so they could not fight again. Egypt did not set out to win an empire through war with other countries. But many cities in the Middle East owed loyalty to Egypt, having been conquered by it. Eventually other countries developed better weapons. Egypt was defeated by the Persians, Greeks and then the Romans, and became part of the Roman Empire.

GLOSSARY

ADZE A tool used in carpentry to plane wood to a smooth finish.

AMULET A lucky charm believed to protect a person from evil or illness.

AWL A carpentry tool used to make holes.

BA The spirit or soul, which the Egyptians believed lived on when a person died.

BISECT To cut in two exactly.

CASTANETS Two curved pieces of wood made to click together to keep time in music.

CHARIOTEER A chariot driver.

DELTA A low-lying marshy area where a river meets the sea, made of sand or mud dropped by the river.

DYNASTY A ruling family.

EMBALMING See mummification.

EXCAVATE To unearth historical remains.

FERTILISER Minerals put on the soil to nourish crops.

HARPOON A type of spear with a long line attached, with which the spear can be retrieved after it is thrown.

HIEROGLYPH A picture symbol. The Egyptian writing system was made up of hieroglyphs.

KA A person's double, who the Egyptians believed stayed with them after death.

KOHL Black eyeliner.

LAPIS LAZULI A valuable blue stone used to colour paintings and sculpture in ancient times.

MUMMIFICATION The process of preserving a dead body so it does not decay.

NATRON A type of salt used to preserve dead bodies in ancient Egypt.

OBELISK A tall stone column with a triangular top.

PAPYRUS A type of reed found by the Nile, used to make paper and many other things.

PHARAOH The name given to the Egyptian ruler.

PITH The inner stem of a plant.

ROUTED Forced to make a disorderly retreat.

SCIMITAR A type of sword with a curving blade.

SCRIBE An official or person whose work involves writing.

SENET A board game played in ancient Egypt, rather like backgammon.

SHADUF A machine used to raise water.

SPATULA A tool with a broad blade, used for spreading.

VENT An opening.

VILLA A fine house, usually in the country.

VIZIER The highest government official in ancient Egypt.

INDEX